The Broons' Burns Night

D0247810

The BURNS FEDERATION

Joe Broon

has been awarded this Certificate of Merit
for Excellence in Recitation
from Scottish Literature

Date 20th January

James Glass

HON. SECRETARY OF SCHOOLS COMPETITIONS

WORD NOTES WILD

BETTER A WEE BUSH THAN 'NAE BIELD

Ref. P.

ROBERT DINWIDDIE & CO LTD DUMFRIES

THeRe once WAS a poeT FRom AYR (shire)
who WAS fond of The Ladies so FAir.
He WROTE TaRBolTon Lassies
And GReen GROW The Rashes
And hUnneRS and hUnneRS mair
by LORD BYRooh

This edition first published 2008 by Waverley Books, an imprint of Geddes & Grosset, David Dale House, New Lanark, Scotland ML11 9DJ

Some material previously published in The Broons' Burns Night, a promotional item given away with the Sunday Post, January 13, 2008.

Text and design copyright © 2008 Waverley Books. The Broons logo and characters appear courtesy of, and copyright © DC Thomson & Co Ltd. Additional artwork by Hugo Breingan.

The Broons and the publisher would like to thank the Burns Federation for giving us Horace's certificate and allowing us to reproduce the other certificates.

ISBN 978-1-902407-71-5

Printed and Bound in the EU

2 3 4 5 6 7 8 9 10

ImpORTInT
biT →

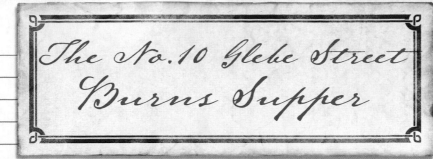

The No.10 Glebe Street Burns Supper

THE BROONS'S BURNS'S
APPREESHEEAYSHUn SOCIETTY

Running Order

1

The Selkirk Grace

First Course

Toasts

Address To The Haggis

Second Course — Haggis,
Tatties and Neeps

Third Course

Pudding

The Immortal Memory

Reading

Song

To the Lassies

Reply

Song

"A man's a man for a that"

Certificate
of
Excellence
Presented
to
Horace Broon
From
The
Robert Burns
WORLD FEDERATION LIMITED

John F. Haining

President

Shirley

Chief E...

Octo...

1885

Burns Night Shopping List

Split peas, barley, beef bone, kail, leek,
onions, carrots, parsnip, neeps, tatties
Haggis (the butcher's ain)
Butter, half pun
Salmon
Oatmeal, pinhead meal
Double cream
Eggs
Raspberries
Flour
Ayrshire Cheese
Oatcakes from Goodfellow's
Whisky

WHY WE CELEBRATE BURNS NIGHT
by Horace Broon 4A

January 25th is Burns Night, the birthday of the poet Robert Burns. He was born in 1759, around 250 years ago, so what is so important about this Scottish writer that we celebrate his birthday in preference to others?

His work has many facets to it. We have Burns the ploughman poet, close to nature and empathising with a helpless animal in "To a Mouse"; we have Burns the political commentator in "A Parcel o' Rogues" and "A Man's a Man for a' That"; Burns the broken-hearted lover in "Ae Fond Kiss"; Burns the satirical comic in "Holy Wullie". He can write as easily and unrepentantly about the sentimental side of life as he can about the bawdy side, the political and the comic, the tragic and the historical. Because of his humble origins he speaks for the common man. Because of his learning and artistry he speaks to the scholar. Because of his experience he speaks for "everyman". His work's range of subject matter, its wide appeal, his talent as an artist and the opportunity, with the popularity of his work, to keep the Scots language alive and in use, mean Burns is as important to Scotland as a nation as he is to Scottish literature. That, in my opinion, is why we still celebrate Burns Night and why we will continue to do so for years to come.

Good answer. However, watch your sentence length, overuse of semicolons and repetition of "because" at the beginning of a sentence. 8/10

5

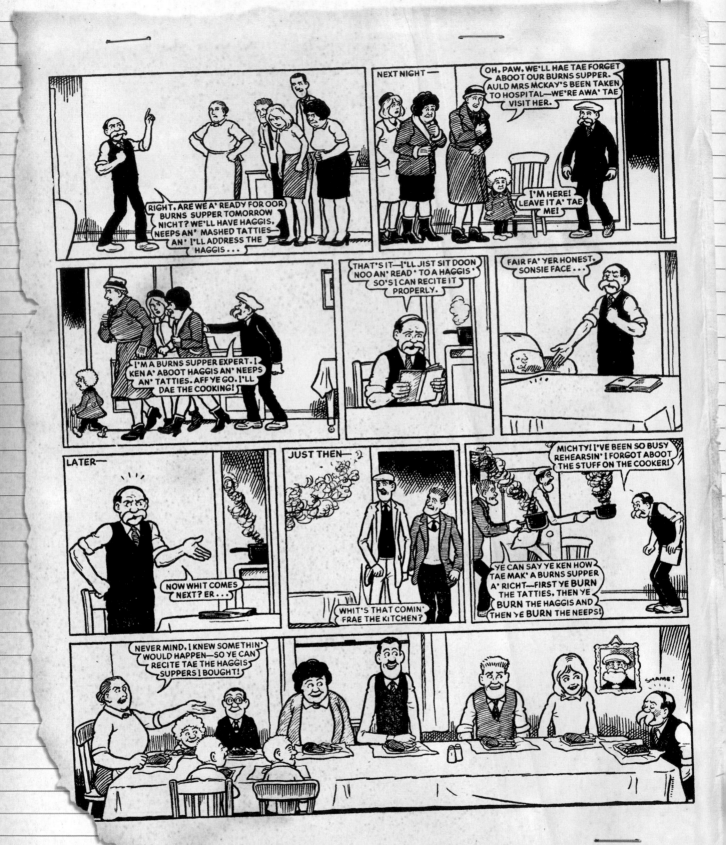

How To Do The
Gay Gordons by Joe

* Choose a partner — difficult for Hen, him being sae tall. He aye ends up wi' wee lassies at the dancin'.
* The best line tae use in approachin' yer partner: "Are ye dancin'?"
  An' she should say: "Are ye askin?"
  An' that should be you wi' a click!
* A' the couples spread aroond the room facing anti-clockwise, lassies on the right.
* If ye are dancin' in the livin' room mak' sure Maw's ornaments are safe or ye'll get intae awfy trouble.
* Likely the bloke in the band or on the record will ca' oot the dance. He is ca'd the Caller!
* The tune will likely be "Scotland the Brave" or "The Gay Gordons".
* This is whit ye dae! Stand side by side, the lassie on the right. Join right hands ower the lassie's shoulder (the man's arm should be behind her back) and left hands joined in front. Walk forward wi' confidence, for fower steps, starting oot on the right foot.
  Still moving in the same direction (and dinnae let go) pivot on the spot clockwise, easin' the lassie around (so ye end up wi' the left hand behind the lassie and the right hand is in front o' her). Then ye tak' fower steps backwards (takin' care no' tae fa' doon).
* Repeat that bit, goin' in the opposite direction — walking forward, then pivot — this time anti-clockwise till ye are back where ye started.
* Then, let go left hands, raise right hands above the lassie's heid. The lassie pivots on the spot. (The man can staun an' admire, or dae a wee dance on the spot.)
  Then ye join hands like in the classic ballroom hold, and polka roond the room till ye fa' or bump into folk like at the dodgems. Rerr!
* Lassies should wear stout shoes and when ye staun' on ither folk's muckle feet, just smile and say "you're a champ dancer". The riposte will likely be: "Aye an' you're a d——n chancer!

A Man's A Man For A' That

Robert Burns

Is there for honest Poverty
    That hings his head, an' a' that;
The coward slave—we pass him by,
    We dare be poor for a' that!
For a' that, an' a' that.
    Our toils obscure an' a' that,
The rank is but the guinea's stamp,
    The man's the gowd for a' that.

What though on hamely fare we dine,
    Wear hoddin grey, an' a' that ;
Gie fools their silks, and knaves their wine;
    A man's a man for a' that:
For a' that, an' a' that,
    Their tinsel show, an' a' that;
The honest man, tho' e'er sae poor,
    Is king o' men for a' that.

Ye see yon birkie, ca'd a lord,
    Wha struts, an' stares, an' a' that;
Tho' hundreds worship at his word,
    He's but a coof for a' that.
For a' that, an' a' that,
    His riband, star, an' a' that.
The man o' independent mind
    He looks an' laughs at a' that.

A prince can mak a belted knight,
    A marquis, duke, an' a' that;
But an honest man's aboon his might,
    Gude faith, he maunna fa' that!
For a' that, an' a' that,
    Their dignities an' a' that,
The pith o' sense, an' pride o' worth,
    Are higher rank than a' that.

Then let us pray that come it may,
    (As come it will for a' that,)
That Sense and Worth, o'er a' the earth,
    May bear the gree, an' a' that.
For a' that, an' a' that,
    It's coming yet for a' that,
That man to man, the world o'er,
    Shall brithers be for a' that.

Ae Fond Kiss

Robert Burns

Ae fond kiss, and then we sev - er! Ae fare - weel, and

D   G   D   A Bmin   G

then for ev - er! Deep in heart - wrung tears I'll pledge thee,

A   D   G   D   G

War - ring sighs and groans I'll wage thee.

D   A7   D   G   D   A   D

Who shall say that Fortune grieves him,
While the star of hope she leaves him?
Me, nae cheerful twinkle lights me,
Dark despair around benights me.

I'll ne'er blame my partial fancy,
Naething could resist my Nancy;
But to see her was to love her,
Love but her, and love for ever.

Had we never loved sae kindly,
Had we never loved sae blindly,
Never met, or never parted,
We had ne'er been broken-hearted!

Fare thee weel, thou first and fairest,
Fare thee weel, thou best and dearest;
Thine be ilka joy and treasure,
Peace, enjoyment, love, and pleasure!

Ae fond kiss, and then we sever!
Ae fareweel, alas! For ever!
Deep in heart-wrung tears I'll pledge thee,
Warring sighs and groans I'll wage thee.

Robert Bruce's March
to Bannockburn
or
Scots, Wha Hae
by
Robert Burns

Scots, wha hae wi' Wallace bled,
Scots, wham Bruce has aften led,
Welcome tae your gory bed,—
    Or to Victorie!

Now's the day, and now's the hour:
See the front o' battle lour,
See approach proud Edward's
  power—
    Chains and Slaverie!—

Wha will be a traitor knave?
Wha will fill a coward's grave?
Wha sae base as be a slave?
    Let him turn and flee!—

Wha, for Scotland's king and law,
Freedom's sword will strongly draw,
Freeman stand, or Freeman fa',
    Let him on wi' me!—

By Oppression's woes and pains!
By your sons in servile chains!
We will drain our dearest veins,
    But they shall be free!

Lay the proud usurpers low!
Tyrants fall in every foe!
Liberty's in every blow! —
    Let us do or dee!'

The Selkirk Grace
by Paw

(... well ... read by Paw ...

written by Robert Burns)

Actually, Paw, it was just attributed to Robert Burns

Some hae meat and canna eat,
And some wad eat that want it;
We hae meat an' we can eat,
And sae the Lord be thankit.

Paw

First Course

STOBSWELL BOWLING CLUB BURNS SUPPER

MENU

The Selkirk Grace

Cock-a-Leekie Soup

Address To A Haggis

Haggis, warm 'n reekin, wi' Champit Tatties, Mashed Neeps and a Wee Dram.

Tipsy Laird

Oatcakes and Ayrshire Cheese

A Tassie o' Coffee and anither Wee Dram

The Immortal Memory

Song: Ca' the Yowes

Holy Wullie

The Lassies

Reply

Song: Is There For Honest Poverty

Vote of Thanks and anither Wee Dram

Daphne's Burns Supper

Why not have food with every toast, poem and song!

Selkirk Grace: Scotch Broth
To the Queen: Fruit Cocktail
To Friends: Oatcakes and Potted Hough
To A Haggis: Haggis, Neeps, Tatties
Immortal Memory: Roast Turkey
Song: Trifle
Recitation: Cheeseboard
Song: Coffee and Shortbread
The Lassies: Liqueurs
Reply to the Laddies: Tablet
Song: Some of Granpaw's Elderberry Wine
Vote of thanks – Er ... sandwiches? Might be hungry again by then.

Cock-a-Leekie Soup

3-lb chicken with giblets
1 bay leaf
1 lb leeks, chopped
4 pints water
1 oz rice
Salt and pepper.

In a large pot, place the whole chicken, the giblets, water, bay leaf, green of the leeks and salt and pepper. Bring tae the boil and then simmer for 2 tae 3 hours. Pierce the flesh of the chicken tae mah' sure it's cooked. Tak' oot the chicken, giblets and the bay leaf. Skim fat fae surface.

Add the rice and the white o' the leeks and cook for 10 minutes. Remove some flesh frae the chicken, add tae the soup and cook 10 minutes mair.

SCOTCH BROTH

1 ¹/₂ lb. neck of mutton
2 oz. barley
2 oz. peas
1 onion
1 leek
¹/₂ small white heart of cabbage
1 cup diced turnip
1 cup diced carrot
1 grated carrot
1 tablespoonful chopped
  parsley
Salt and pepper
4 pints water

Wash the peas and soak overnight. Wipe and trim the meat, and put into the broth-pot with cold water, peas, barley, and salt. Bring to the boil and skim.

Cut up the leek and onion and add along with the diced turnip and carrot. Simmer slowly for three to four hours.

Add the shredded cabbage and grated carrot, and simmer an hour longer. Just before serving, add the parsley.

Add pepper and more salt if required, and serve hot.

Ye Banks and Braes o' Bonnie Doon

Robert Burns

Oft ha'e I roved by bonnie Doon
To see the rose and woodbine twine;
And ilka bird sang o' its love,
And fondly sae did I o' mine.
Wi' lightsome heart I pu'd a rose,
Fu' sweet upon its thorny tree:
But my fause lover stole my rose,
But Ah! he left the thorn wi' me.

14

Lentil Soup

4 oz lentils
1 oz vegetable oil
3 oz carrots
2 oz turnips
1 onion
1 large potato
2 pints water
1 ham hough
Black pepper

Add the water to the pot and the ham hough and bring tae the boil. Simmer for around 2 hours, after which you should remove the ham hough, strain and reserve the stock, and skim off any fat. When cool, remove some of the meat from the ham hough for adding to the soup later.

Wash the lentils and dice the vegetables.

Pour a little vegetable oil into a large pot and cook the vegetables over a low heat with the lid on for around 10 minutes.

Add the lentils and the stock and simmer for about 2 hours. Add the meat from the ham hough to the soup and heat through. Taste, season and serve.

Cullen Skink

A delicious fish soup

*1 onion, sliced or chopped
3 or 4 crushed peppercorns
butter
water
1 medium Finnan haddie
(salted smoked haddock)
500 g/1 lb (approx.) potatoes
600 ml/1 pint milk
salt and pepper*

Fry the onions with some butter and the crushed peppercorns. Add the fish, cover with water and cook until the skin becomes loose enough to remove. Remove the skin and break the fish into flakes, removing the fish bones as you do this. Put the haddock aside and return the skin and bones to the pan and simmer for about an hour to make a stock.

Boil and mash the potatoes. Strain the fish stock, add to a large pan and simmer with the milk. Add as much potato as you like, depending on whether you prefer thick or thin soup. Add the flaked haddock. Season with salt and pepper and perhaps some butter.

Serves approx. three to four

Housewife Weekly
"cut out and keep"
Scottish Recipes

No.27

POTTED HOUGH

1-lb shin of beef
2-lb beef shin bone or
　　knuckle of veal
1 teaspoon salt
$1/2$ teaspoon allspice berries
$1/2$ mace blade
$1/2$ teaspoon peppercorns
1 bay leaf
Salt
Pepper

Place the meat and bone in a large pot and pour in enough cold water to just cover it. Tie the bay leaf and spices in a piece of muslin and add this to the pot. Bring to the boil and then reduce the heat and simmer for three to four hours. Drain the stock from the pan but don't throw it away. Flake the meat from the bone and shred or chop it finely. Place the stock and meat back in the pan and taste. Season. Boil again for another 10 minutes or so to reduce the liquid. Pour the mixture into moulds or bowls and leave to cool completely. Chill. Serve with bread or oatcakes.

Fruit Cocktail

2 grapefruits
3 oranges
1 melon
1 oz. crystallised ginger

Cut grapefruits and oranges in half and cut off the peel. Slice out the flesh from the segments into a bowl. Cut melon in half, remove seeds and ball or slice flesh. Chop ginger finely and add to the bowl. Mix. Chill at least 1 hour. Serve as a course to refresh the palate.

No.21

Housewife Weekly
"cut out and keep"
Scottish Recipes

Oatcakes - Perfect with cheese, butter, honey or jam

*100 g/4 oz coarse oatmeal
100 g/4 oz medium oatmeal
100 g/4 oz fine oatmeal or barley meal
1/4 teaspoon baking powder
1/2 teaspoon salt
25 g/1 oz butter or dripping, melted
4 to 7 teaspoons boiling water*

Preheat the oven to Mark 4/300°F/150°C. Mix the oatmeal. Put 250 g/9 oz of the oatmeal, the baking powder and salt into a bowl and stir in the melted butter. Slowly add the hot water to make a smooth, firm paste.

Form into a ball and roll the mixture on a table sprinkled with 25 g/1 oz of the remaining oatmeal. Ensure the mixture is completely covered with oats and roll out into a circle about 1/2 cm (1/8 inch) thick. Cut into 8 wedges. Using a fish slice, transfer the wedges on to a baking sheet covered in the remaining oatmeal.

Bake in the centre of the oven for about 30 minutes without allowing to brown.

Makes eight oatcakes

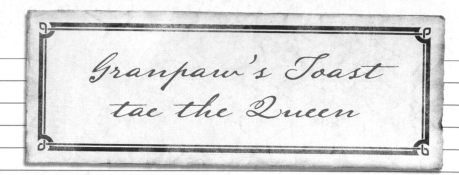

Granpaw's Toast tae the Queen

Afore the haggis arrives ... here is a toast to Her Majesty, Queen Elizabeth 11. Lang live the Queen, and lang may yer lum reek, Ma'am!

An' here is a toast tae oor very own Queen o' Glebe Street ... Maw:

   Thank you, Maw for a' yer fine cookin'
   Yer no as green as yer cabbage lookin'.
   Tonight's guid eatin' is thanks to you,
    So enjoy yersel' whatever ye do.
   Yer clootie dumpling tastes divine,
   (But yer mince is no' as guid as mine).

   Here's a toast to lovely Maw ...
   My very favourite daughter-in-law!

TATTIE SOUP

8-10 potatoes
1 2 onions
3 large carrots, grated
A mutton bone
4 pints water
Salt and pepper
1 tablespoon chopped parsley

Early in the day, wash the mutton bone and put it into a pot with cold water and salt. Boil the bone for stock. Bone stock needs to cook for 5 hours. Wash, peel, and slice the potatoes. Wash, scrape, and grate the carrot. Peel and cut up the onion. Remove the bone and strain the bone stock. Add the vegetables to this stock in the pot, and simmer for 1^1/$_2$ to 2 hours. Wash and chop the parsley, and add to the soup right at the end. Season, and serve. Serves 4 to 6 approx

How to Learn a Poem Aff by Heart by Horace

I recite poems at oor Burns Suppers sometimes. These are my handy tips aboot learnin' poems:

- Write it oot! Copy it oot on a bit o' paper, word-for-word, line-for-line, wi a' the commas and full stops.
- Keep it handy so ye can read it anywhere — on the bus or in the bathtub.
- Read the whole thing through quite a few times to get the hang o' the whole thing. Then dae it again.
- Read it oot loud, so ye can hear how a' the words sound.
- Have a real guid look at it, and mak' sure ye understand the words — there will be big words, an' wee yins tae, that ye micht no' ken.
- Imagine pictures in yer heid o' what ye are readin'.
- Once ye have read it a few more times, see if ye can mak' a recording in ane o' thae record booths, or a tape so ye can play it tae yerself. Yer ain voice sounds richt funny sometimes!
- If the poem ye are learnin' is awfy long, an' not broken up into wee verses, mark it every four lines, and only try to learn four at a time.
- Withoot lookin' at the paper, try and say the first and second lines, and then the third and fourth. Ye can look at yer paper tae remind ye if ye cannae get it right. Then after ye hae done four lines, go on to the next four.
- Get a pal tae listen to ye — give them the bit o' paper — and if ye get stuck they can prompt ye with a word tae get ye goin' again.
- Wherever ye go, recite the poem to yersel'. Beware o' disturbin' folk on the bus, or ye micht get skelped! A lot o' folk dinna understand poets or poetry!
- An' just afore ye put yer heid on the pillow at nicht, recite it again. A lot o' folk say it's a scientific fact that ye remember what ye read just afore ye go tae sleep.
- Even when ye are sure ye ken the poem by heart, keep that wee piece o' paper in yer pocket — 'cause ye'll mibbe hae a wee panic just before ye are due to perform.

When Horace gets ready for school
His school bag is usually full
Of books of hard sums,
Bags of sweeties and gum
He's a geek but the boy is no fool
if he left them we'd eat them a'!

19

Hen's Toast to Absent Friends

Here's a toast to those who canna be here.

To a' oor pals no longer wi' us, God bless you – we miss you. Granmaw Broon, a toast to you: we miss your scones and steak pie, and the way you chased me and Joe roond the scullery when we gave you cheek – it never really did me any harm, though I canna speak for Joe. To the gossipy Gows: I hope yer enjoying yer spam the night! To wee Jeannie McAllister: I bet your date wi' you Bruiser McIntyre is no' as much fun as oor Burns night is going to be!

Join me, everyone, in a toast to absent friends!

The Twins' Toast to Absent Scones

O lovely scones youl were sae glid
maw made youl yesterday
now yoov all gone we don't feel bad
youl're still with us in a way
we ate youl when maw went to bed
hee hee hee hee hee

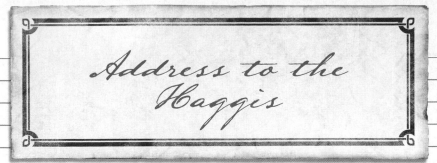

Address to the Haggis

By Robert Burns

Fair fa' your honest, sonsie face,
  Great chieftain o' the puddin'-
     race!
Aboon them a' ye tak' your place,
     Painch, tripe, or thairm:
Weel are ye wordy of a grace
     As lang's my arm.

The groaning trencher there ye
     fill,
Your hurdies like a distant hill,
Your pin wad help to mend a mill
     In time o' need,
While thro' your pores the dews distil
     Like amber bead.

His knife see rustic Labour dight,
An cut you up wi' ready slieght,
Trenching your gushing entrails
     bright,
     Like onie ditch;
And then, O what a glorious sight,
     Warm-reekin', rich!

Then, horn for horn, they stretch an'
     strive:
Deil tak the hindmost, on they drive,
Till a' their weel-swall'd kytes belyve
     Are bent like drums;
The auld Guidman, maist like to rive,
     'Bethankit!' hums.

Is there that owre his French *ragout*,
Or *olio* that wad staw a sow,
Or *fricassee* wad mak her spew
     Wi' perfect sconner,
  Looks down wi' sneering, scornfu'
     view
     On sic a dinner?

Poor devil! see him owre his trash,
As feckless as a wither'd rash,
His spindle shank a guid whip-lash,
     His nieve a nit;
Thro' bloody flood or field to dash,
     O how unfit!

But mark the Rustic, haggis-fed,
The trembling earth resounds his
     tread,
Clap in his walie nieve a blade,
     He'll make it whissle;
An legs an' arms, an' heads will sned,
     Like taps o' thrissle.

Ye Pow'rs, wha mak mankind your
     care,
And dish them out their bill o' fare,
Auld Scotland wants nae skinking
     ware
     That jaups in luggies:
But, if ye wish her gratefu' prayer,
     Gie her a Haggis!

Why do pipers walk while they play?

To get away from the noise!

THE BUT AN' BEN BURNS SUPPER

The Selkirk Grace (Paw)

Scotch Broth

Address To A Haggis
(Hen, with Me on the pipes)

Haggis
Champit Tatties, Mashed Neeps, Skirlie
A Wee Dram

Steak Pie

Athole Brose

Coffee, Tea, Taiblet, and A Wee Dram

Granpaw's Elderberry Wine

The Immortal Memory (Horace)

Tam O'Shanter (Paw)

Song: Ca' the Yowes (Maw)

Song: O' Whistle and I Will Come Tae Ye
My Lad (Daphne)

The Lassies (Granpaw)

Reply (Maggie)

Song: The Star O' Rabbie Burns
(The Twins)

A wee song fae the Bairn
(and Anither Wee Dram)

burns supper– that's whit paw does ha! ha!

Haggis

8 oz sheep's liver
4 oz beef suet
2 large onions
4 oz toasted oatmeal
Salt and pepper

Boil liver in pan of water for 40 minutes. Retain water and remove liver and mince it finely.

Roughly chop onions and cook on a low heat in a frying pan with a little suet. Once cooked, chop them finely with the rest of the suet.

Toast oatmeal.

Combine ingredients in a bowl and season with salt and pepper. Moisten mixture using liquid in which liver was cooked.

Press mixture into a pudding basin, cover top with foil and place in large pot of water, and boil for 2 hours.

haggis

Holy Willie's† Prayer

And send the godly in a pet to pray."— POPE

O Thou, that in the heavens does dwell,
Wha, as it pleases best Thysel',
Sends ane to Heaven an' ten to Hell,
  A' for Thy glory,
And no for ony guid or ill
  They've done afore Thee!

I bless and praise Thy matchless might,
When thousands Thou hast left in night,
That I am here afore Thy sight,
  For gifts an' grace,
A burnin' and a shinin' light
  To a' this place.—

What was I, or my generation,
That I should get sic exaltation?
I wha deserv'd most just damnation
  For broken laws,
Sax thousand years 'ere my creation,
  Thro' Adam's cause!

When from my mither's womb I fell,
Thou might hae plung'd me deep in hell,
To gnash my gooms, and weep and wail,
  In burnin lakes,
Where damnèd devils roar and yell,
  Chain'd to their stakes.—

Yet I am here a chosen sample,
To show thy grace is great and ample;
I'm here a pillar o' Thy temple,
  Strong as a rock,
A guide, a buckler, and example,
  To a' Thy flock. —

O Lord, Thou kens what zeal I bear,
When drinkers drink, an' swearers swear,
An' singing here, an' dancin there,
  Wi' great and sma';
For I am keepit by Thy fear
  Free frae them a'.

But yet, O Lord! confess I must,
At times I'm fash'd wi' fleshly lust;
An' sometimes, too, in worldly trust,
  Vile Self gets in;
But Thou remembers we are dust,
  Defil'd wi' sin.

O Lord!—yestreen, Thou kens, wi' Meg—
Thy pardon I sincerely beg;
O may't ne'er be a livin' plague
  To my dishonour,
An' I'll ne'er lift a lawless leg
  Again upon her.—

Besides, I farther maun avow,
Wi' Leezie's lass, three times I trow—
But Lord, that Friday I was fou,
  When I cam near her;
Or else, Thou kens, Thy servant true
  Wad ne'er hae steer'd her.—

Maybe Thou lets this fleshly thorn
Beset Thy servant e'en and morn,
Lest he, owre proud and high shou'd turn,
  That he's sae gifted;
If sae, Thy han' maun e'en be borne,
  Until Thou lift it. —

Lord, bless Thy chosen in this place,
For here Thou has a chosen race!
But God confound their stuborn face,
  An' blast their name,
Wha bring Thy elders to disgrace
  An' open shame. —

Lord, mind Gaw'n Hamilton's deserts;
He drinks, an' swears, an' plays at cartes,
Yet has sae mony takin' arts,
  Wi' great an' sma',
Frae God's ain priest the people's hearts
  He steals awa'.

And when we chasten'd him therefore,
Thou kens how he bred sic a splore,
And set the warld in a roar
  O' laughing at us;—
Curse Thou his basket and his store,
  Kail an' potatoes.

Lord, hear my earnest cry and pray'r,
Against that Presbyt'ry o' Ayr;
Thy strong right hand, Lord make it bare
  Upon their heads;
Lord visit them, an' dinna spare,
  For their misdeeds.

†Holy Willie: William Fisher, a hypocritical elder in Mauchline

O Lord my God! that glib-tongued Aitken,
My vera heart an' flesh are quakin,
To think how we stood sweatin, shakin,
    An' p—'d wi' dread,
While he, wi' hingin lip an' snakin,
    Held up his head.

Lord, in Thy day o' vengeance try him,
Lord, visit them wha did employ him,
And pass not in Thy mercy by them,
    Nor hear their prayer,
But for Thy people's sake destroy them,
    An' dinna spare.

But, Lord, remember me an' mine
Wi' mercies temporal and divine,
That I for grace an' gear may shine,
    Excell'd by nane,
And a' the glory shall be Thine,
    Amen, Amen!

Vegetarian Haggis

½ lb. of flour
½ lb. of breadcrumbs
6 oz. of butter
A small onion chopped
A teacupful of pinhead oatmeal
½ cup of cooked lentils
2 Eggs
Vegetable stock

Melt butter, add to the dry ingredients and moisten with a little stock. Season with white pepper and a little salt to taste. Boil in a covered pudding basin for about 3 hours.

We dinna like haggis made oot of Vegetinarians

SKIRLIE

2 oz butter or dripping
1 onion, chopped
3 ½ oz medium or coarse oatmeal
Salt and pepper

Melt the butter in a frying pan and fry the onion until soft but not too crispy. Then add the oatmeal gradually and stir till all the butter is absorbed.

Serve hot as an accompaniment to meats or haggis or as a stuffing for roasts.

Clapshot
from Mrs Frame

1 lb floury tatties, boiled
1 lb turnip, chopped and boiled
1 onion, fried
2 tbsps chopped chives   serves 4
Salt and pepper
3 oz butter

Boil the tatties and turnip. Gently fry the chopped onions in 25 g/1 oz butter until soft but not brown. Mash the boiled potato and boiled turnip together with the remaining butter and the fried onions. Once mashed, mix in the chopped chives and the seasoning. Serve hot with oatcakes or as an accompaniment to haggis.

Lang Kail

Take twa or three stalks o' fresh crisp young green kail, separate the blades frae the stalk, wash well, shred it finely and boil till tender in salted water. This could take 20 minutes, but keep testing it. Drain and beat up the leaves wi plenty o' butter, salt and pepper. Serve wi' meat.

Champit Tatties with Syboes

8 medium potatoes (peeled)
Small bunch of spring onions
1/4 pt milk
Salt and pepper
A dod of butter per person

Boil the potatoes until they are soft. Drain and return them to the heat to dry slightly before mashing. Finely chop the white and green of the spring onions and cook in the milk. Beat this mixture into the mashed potatoes until they are fluffy and smooth. Season to taste and serve a generous helping onto each plate, topping with a dod of butter.

Steak Pie

2 lb stewing steak

1 tablespoon seasoned plain flour

2 oz dripping

1 large onion, chopped

3 large carrots

1 pint beef stock

Worcestershire sauce

9 oz puff pastry

Toss the steak in the seasoned flour. Melt the dripping in a large saucepan and brown the meat, and then remove and put aside. Fry the onions and the carrots until softened slightly and then return the meat tae the pan. Add a couple o' dashes o' Worcestershire sauce, black pepper and salt tae the beef stock, and pour into the pan. Cover and bring tae the boil, then reduce the heat and simmer, still covered, for twa hours, checking noo and again. (When cooked, ye can put it aside tae cool, have a wee dram, and mak' the pie the next day!) Pour the stew into a 3-pint ashet. Roll out the pastry and press down firmly around the sides of the ashet and on top of the stew. Brush the top wi' beaten egg or some milk and score into criss-crosses. Mak' a hole in the centre tae let the steam oot. Cook for 30 minutes in the centre o' a hot oven.

Roast Shoulder o' Lamb

Stuffing:

Cup of bread crumbs

1/2 cup suet

1 tablespoon parsley

Mixed herbs

Grated rind of lemon and the juice

1/2 teaspoon salt

Pepper, less than 1/2 teaspoon

Yolk of egg

4 lb shoulder of lamb

Cook 15 minutes in a hot oven then 40 minutes tae each pound in a moderate oven.

Place a' the dry ingredients in a small basin and add lemon juice and egg. Wipe the mutton, take out the bones and spread the stuffing over it. Tie it up, and untie once cooked. The oven should be very hot. Place in the oven on a dish within a tin filled wi'' water. After 15 minutes, reduce heat to moderate. Pour dripping over the roast and baste frequently. Untie. Serve with mint sauce, peas and new potatoes.

Beef Olives

1 lb. steak
1 oz. dripping
Salt and pepper
3/4 pt. water
1 oz. flour
Carrot and turnip
  Stuffing:
2 oz. bread crumbs
1 teasp. chopped parsley
1 oz. chopped suet
Salt and pepper
Milk to bind

MIX stuffing into a stiff paste. Cut steak into strips 2 in. wide, put 1 teasp. mixture on each, roll up and tie with string. Brown well in hot fat, pour off surplus fat. Add boiling water and simmer 3/4 hour. Add sliced vegetables and cook 3/4 hour or until tender. Remove string from olives, season, and thicken gravy. Serve neatly on a hot ashet.

Roast Chicken

A stuffed bird takes longer to cook. You can cook some stuffing separately if you cook it in a covered oven dish. Give a chicken 20 minutes per pound in a hot oven, and another 20 minutes for good measure.

A large chicken
Stuffing: 3 oz. breadcrumbs, 2 oz. suet, a few leaves of parsley (chopped), pepper and salt, and 1 egg

Prepare the chicken, take out the giblets — or get the butcher to do it. Wash the chicken and coat in butter. Make the stuffing. Draw up the legs under the wings and stuff the chicken's breast. Place a buttered paper over the bird, and baste frequently. Roast in a hot oven for at least 1 hour. Pierce the flesh and if the juice runs clear it is cooked. If not, cook for longer. Serve with clear gravy, roast potatoes and bread sauce.

The Broons
Burns Nicht

Bill O' Fare

Cullen Skink

Haggis
Neeps
Tatties and Syboes

Roast Shoulder of Lamb

Cranachan

Caramel Shortbread
Coffee and Tea
Whisky

Grilled Scottish Salmon

A delicious, simple way to eat fresh Scottish salmon

No.33

wild Scottish salmon steak about 4 cm/1 1/2 inches thick
vegetable oil
25 g/1 oz butter, melted
chopped parsley
chopped dill
lemon juice

Dip the steak in melted butter or vegetable oil, sprinkle with salt and place under a hot grill until the flesh changes colour. Turn the steak and cook the other side. Serve with the central bone removed.

For a sauce, melt a little butter, add dill, parsley, a squeeze of lemon juice and pour around the steak. Serve with boiled potatoes and shelled or sugar-snap peas.

Serves one

Housewife Weekly
"cut out and keep"
Scottish Recipes

cut here

Granpaw's Burns Night Tips

At the bowlin' club we hae a piper tae welcome a'body arrivin'. If ye cannae pay a piper, mak' yer ain music. Yon Andy Stewart has braw records that ye can play.

At the proper suppers, the piper keeps playin' till the Top Table is ready tae sit doon, then the piper gets a clap.

Ye'll hae tae stand up when the haggis gets piped in tae the room — mair clappin'.

First, in comes the cook, and the piper, then whoever is goin' tae address the haggis comes in at their back.

Ye keep clappin' in time till a'body at the Top Table sits doon, and the piper stops. Then ye can a' sit doon.

Listen tae the Address — the guid bit comes when ye hear "His knife see rustic labour dight" when the knife gets plunged intae the haggis. If ye are near the front — mind no' tae get splashed wi' hot grease — it can fair fly aboot.

When ye hear "Gie her a haggis!" that's the end o' that bit — and time for eating!

The TWins' BuRns nighT Tips

BuRns nighT Tips can be made by helping cleaR up dinner dishes while The oldeR folk enjoy a 'RefReshminT'. The moRe 'RefReshminT' enjoyed The moRe geneRus They become - espeshally folk you aRe no' RelaTed Tae

Pudding

Trifle

6 sponge cakes
Raspberry jam
5 oz almond biscuits
6 tablespoons sherry
2 soup bowls of raspberries
1 pint of cream custard
10 fl oz double cream, whipped

Spread the sponges with raspberry jam and place in the bottom of a glass trifle bowl. Break up the almond biscuits and sprinkle over the sponges. On top of this pour 6 tablespoons of sherry. On top of this spread the raspberries. If the custard is cooled then pour it over the raspberries and chill.
Spread with whipped cream and cover with flaked almonds.
   Serves about six, so we have to make three!

Cranachan or Cream Crowdie

Double cream
Coarse toasted oatmeal
Castor sugar
Rum or vanilla
Fresh seasonal berries

Toast some oatmeal lightly in the oven, or in a thick-bottome frying-pan over a gentle heat. This gives it a nutty taste. Bea a bowlful of cream to a stiff froth, and stir in a handful two of oatmeal, making it not too substantial, i.e., the crea must predominate. Sweeten to taste, and flavour with ru or vanilla seeds.
   Throw in a few handfuls of fresh ripe berries—strawberrie blaeberries, raspberries, brambles, or others.

Honey Cake

250 g (8 oz) plain flour
1 tsp cinnamon
1/2 tsp mixed spice
1/2 tsp bicarbonate of soda
125 g (4 oz) butter
125 g (4 oz) brown sugar
1 egg, separated
125g (4 oz) honey
milk to mix
a little caster sugar

Preheat the oven to gas mark 4, 175°C, 350°F. Sieve the flour, spices and bicarbonate together. Cream the butter and brown sugar and beat in the egg yolk. Add the honey to this mixture. Fold in the dry ingredients gradually and gently, adding milk if the mixture is too thick. Whisk the egg white until stiff and fold gently into the mixture.
   Grease or line a loaf tin and pour in the mixture evenly. Sprinkle the top with a little caster sugar so that the cake has a slightly crunchy surface.
   Bake for approximately 30 minutes and test with a skewer. Dredge with more caster sugar when baked.

serve hot or cold.

Meringues – The Basics
Egg whites

Caster sugar (2oz for every egg white)

Use a totally grease-free glass or ceramic bowl (clean with vinegar or lemon juice to make sure). If any yolk gets in the white when you separate them your meringues won't work, so be careful. If you wish to avoid a chewy centre add 1/8 teaspoon of cream of tartar per egg white to unbeaten egg whites. (I like the chewy bit.) 2 egg whites will make about 6 meringues. Whip the egg whites to soft dry peaks. Use an electric mixer or you are in for a lot of work! Don't add the sugar till the eggs are properly whipped. Use no less than 2oz white sugar per egg white, then beat carefully to firm peaks. Wet (do not grease) a baking sheet and flour it. Pipe or spoon the mixture in round blobs onto the sheet. Bake at 200°F (100°C) for about 1½ hrs. Turn off oven but leave them in there overnight without opening the door.

Athole Brose

An indulgent and delicious creamy dessert

100 g/4 oz of toasted coarse or medium oatmeal (reserve 10 g/1/2 oz for garnish)
2 tbsps heather honey
125 ml/1/4 pint whisky
250 ml/1/2 pint double cream
fresh Scottish raspberries as garnish

Preheat the oven to Mark 6/400°F/200°C. Spread the oatmeal evenly over the bottom of a baking tin or tray and toast in the centre of the oven, shaking the tin occasionally, for about 15 minutes, until the oats are a rich golden brown. Add the honey and the whisky to 90 g/31/2 oz of the oats. Whip the cream until it reaches a stiff consistency. Fold in the oats mixture and serve in dessert glasses with a light sprinkling of the remaining toasted oats, some fresh raspberries and a finger of shortbread.

Serves four

Housewife Weekly
"cut out and keep"
Scottish Recipes
No.8

APPLE PUDDING

8 ozs. flour
4 ozs. suet
1 tsp. salt
1 tbsp. baking powder
A little water
Sliced dessert apples
2 tbsps. sugar

Chop the suet and rub into flour. Mix with enough water to make a stiff dough. Line a basin with suet pastry. Fill to the top with sliced apples and sprinkle with sugar. Cover with a suet pastry lid. Cover the basin with some greased paper. If you are boiling, tie with a pudding cloth also. Boil or steam for 2 ½ or 3 hours.

piper

Clootie Dumpling

This is Eileen Smith's recipe. Awfy fine!

6 oz SR flour
6 oz brown breadcrumbs
6 oz suet
1 teaspoon bicarb o' soda
2 teaspoons cinnamon
2 teaspoons ginger
4 oz currants
6 oz sultanas
4 oz soft, dark brown
   sugar
2 tablespoons syrup
Approx 1 1/2 cups milk

Place your cloot in boiling water to sterilise.

Mix all the ingredients together wi' the milk tae mak' a fairly soft consistency. Mak' sure it is weel mixed.

Tak' the cloot oot o' the water an' wring it, then lay it flat oot an' dredge weel wi' flour. Smooth the flour ower wi' your hands tae get an even spread. Place the mix on the cloot, leave room for expansion, tie wi' string. Simmer for 2-3 hours in large pan.

Tak oot o' pot, put in a colander untie string, place plate over an' turn oot. No need tae dry aff.

Serve hot wi' syrup and custard or cold wi' a cuppa!

The Immortal Memory
by Horace

January 25th is Burns Night, the birthday of Scotland's most famous poet, Robert Burns. He is more than our national poet; he has become a symbol of Scottish national identity whose work is still read, recited and sung in schoolrooms, Burns Suppers and concerts all around the world.

Burns was born in 1759, the eldest son of an Alloway farmer, in a two-roomed thatched cottage in the village of Alloway, about two miles from the town of Ayr. The cottage was built by his father, William Burns (also spelled as Burnes) and it survives to this day.

Farming life was very hard and the children worked as hard as the adults. Some believe this hard work in all weathers, contributed to Robert's ill health in later life. His family led a very frugal, physically demanding existence and the young Burns wrote poetry as an escape from these circumstances. Robert was taught at home by a hired teacher and by his father, but his inspiration to be a poet is more likely to have come from his mother, Agnes Broun (surely some relation to us Broons!). Although she could not read, Agnes knew many traditional poems and tales.

She also loved singing and their home would ring to the sound of traditional songs and tunes. Another important influence in his early years was Betty Davidson, a relative of Agnes's. Her tales of ghosts, fairies and witches were to influence Robert Burns's greatest long poem, "Tam O' Shanter". Of course, other important influences in his writing included the women in his life, of which there were many, including his formidable wife Jean Armour, who became the inspiration for so many of his poems.

By his mid—twenties he had become an accomplished writer of verse, publishing his first work, <u>Poems Chiefly in the Scottish Dialect</u>, in 1786. His work shows an acute insight into human behaviour, often reflecting his own fiery political views and demonstrating a great talent for caricature and satire. It also shows irony and wit, unashamed romanticism and sentiment, bawdy humour, a seemingly indiscriminate admiration for the fairer sex and a capacity for compassion and feeling for his fellow man.

Burns died on July 21st, 1796, of rheumatic fever, but he had led a full life in his 37 years. A celebrity and a prolific poet, he left behind a body of work that is undiminished in importance.

Please be upstanding and drink a toast to the immortal memory of Scotland's bard Robert Burns.

TO A MOUSE
ON TURNING HER UP IN HER NEST
WITH THE PLOUGH, NOVEMBER 1785

To a Mouse *was probably composed as Burns worked at the plough (it is said that he did much of his composition this way) and is inspired by a real incident. The poet's mood expresses his doubts about the future and regrets about the past. It may in some way have been influenced by the death of his ten-year-old brother John the month before, and the death of his father the previous year.*

Wee, sleekit, cowrin, tim'rous beastie,
O' what a panic's in thy breastie!
Thou need na start awa sae hasty
    Wi' bickering brattle!
I wad be laith to rin an' chase thee,
    Wi' murd'ring pattle!

I'm truly sorry man's dominion
Has broken Nature's social union,
An' justifies that ill opinion
    Which makes thee startle
At me, thy poor, earth-born companion
    An' fellow mortal!

I doubt na, whyles, but thou may thieve;
What then? poor beastie, thou maun live!
A daimen icker in a thrave
    'S a sma' request;
I'll get a blessin wi' the lave,
    An' never miss't!

Thy wee-bit housie, too, in ruin!
Its silly wa's the win's are strewin!
An' naething, now, to big a new ane,
    O' foggage green!
An' bleak December's win's ensuin,
    Baith snell an' keen!

Thou saw the fields laid bare an' waste,
An' weary winter comin fast,
An' cozie here, beneath the blast,
    Thou thought to dwell,
Till crash! the cruel coulter past
    Out through thy cell.

That wee bit heap o' leaves an' stibble,
Has cost thee monie a weary nibble!
Now thou's turned out, for a' thy trouble,
    But house or hald,
To thole the winter's sleety dribble,
    An' cranreuch cauld!

But Mousie, thou art no thy lane,
In proving foresight may be vain:
The best-laid schemes o' mice an' men
    Gang aft agley,
An' lea'e us nought but grief an' pain,
    For promis'd joy!

Still thou art blest, compared wi' me!
The present only toucheth thee:
But och! I backward cast my e'e,
    On prospects drear!
An' forward, though I canna see,
    I guess an' fear!

BURNS NICHT
AT GRANPAW'S HOOSE

RUNNING ORDER

The Selkirk Grace: Granpaw

The Queen: Paw

To Absent Friends: Joe

The Pipes: Joe

Accordion: Davey fae Newport

Address To The Haggis: Horace

The Immortal Memory: Hen

Song: "Ae Fond Kiss" by Maggie

OOR ~~Holy~~ Wullie: Granpaw

The Lassies: Paw

Reply: Maw

To A Mouse: The Twins

Song: "My Love is Like a Red, Red Rose" by
   Daphne

Song: "Scots, Wha' Hae" by Everybody

MENU

Whisky (Ginger Wine for the bairns)

Tattie Soup

Haggis and Neeps

Beef Olives, Roast Tatties and Lang Kail

Tipsy Laird

Soda Bannocks, Oatcakes and Crowdie cheese

Shortbread

My Hame-made Wine -

Mystery Fruit and Vintage (label fell aff)

TOP TIP:
WARM THE
KNIVES —
THEN
GRANPAW
CANNA TAK
OWER MUCH
BUTTER

39

TAM O' SHANTER
A TALE

By Robert Burns

Of Brownyis and Bogillis full is this Buke.
GAVIN DOUGLAS

When chapman billies leave the street,
An drouthy neebors neebors meet;
As market days are wearing late,
An' folk begin to tak the gate;
While we sit bousing at the nappy,
An' getting fou and unco happy,
We think na on the lang Scots miles,
The mosses, waters, slaps, and styles,
That lie between us and our hame,
Whare sits our sulky, sullen dame,
Gathering her brows like gathering
storm,
Nursing her wrath to keep it warm.

This truth fand honest Tam o' Shanter,
As he frae Ayr ae night did canter:
(Auld Ayr, wham ne'er a town surpasses,
For honest men and bonie lasses.)
O Tam! had'st thou but been sae wise,
As taen thy ain wife Kate's advice!
She tauld thee weel thou was a skellum,
A blethering, blustering, drunken blellum;
That frae November till October,
Ae market day thou was na sober;
That ilka melder wi' the miller,
Thou sat as lang as thou had siller;
That ev'ry naig was ca'd a shoe on,
The smith and thee gat roaring fou on;
That at the Lord's house, even on Sunday,
Thou drank wi' Kirkton Jean till Monday.
She prophesied, that, late or soon,
Thou would be found deep drown'd in
Doon,
Or catch'd wi' warlocks in the mirk
By Alloway's auld, haunted kirk.

Ah! gentle dames, it gars me greet,
To think how monie counsels sweet,
How monie lengthen'd, sage advices
The husband frae the wife despises!

But to our tale:—Ae market-night,
Tam had got planted unco right,
Fast by an ingle, bleezing finely,
Wi' reaming swats, that drank divinely;
And at his elbow, Souter Johnny,

His ancient, trusty, drouthy crony:
Tam lo'ed him like a very brither;
They had been fou for weeks thegither.
The night drave on wi' sangs and clatter;
And ay the ale was growing better:
The landlady and Tam grew gracious
Wi' secret favours, sweet and precious:
The Souter tauld his queerest stories;
The landlord's laugh was ready chorus:
The storm without might rair and rustle,
Tam did na mind the storm a whistle.

Care, mad to see a man sae happy,
E'en drown'd himsel amang the nappy.
As bees flee hame wi' lades o' treasure,
The minutes wing'd their way wi' pleas-
ure:
Kings may be blest but Tam was glorious,
O'er a' the ills o' life victorious!

But pleasures are like poppies
spread:
You seize the flow'r, its bloom is shed;
Or like the snow falls in the river,
A moment white—then melts for ever;
Or like the Borealis race,
That flit ere you can point their place;
Or like the rainbow's lovely form
Evanishing amid the storm.
Nae man can tether time or tide;
The hour approaches Tam maun ride:
That hour, o'night's black arch the
key-stane,
That dreary hour Tam mounts his beast
in;
And sic a night he taks the road in,
As ne'er poor sinner was abroad in.

The wind blew as 'twad blawn its
last;
The rattling showers rose on the blast;
The speedy gleams the darkness
swallow'd;
Loud, deep, and lang the thunder
bellow'd:
That night, a child might understand,
The Deil had business on his hand.

Weel mounted on his grey meare
Meg,
A better never lifted leg,
Tam skelpit on through dub and mire,
Despising wind, and rain, and fire;
Whiles holding fast his guid blue bonnet,
Whiles crooning o'er some auld Scots
sonnet,
Whiles glow'ring round wi' prudent cares,
Lest bogles catch him unawares:
Kirk-Alloway was drawing nigh,
Whares ghaists and houlets nightly cry.

By this time he was cross the ford,
Whare in the snaw the chapman smoor'd;
And past the birks and meikle stane,
Whare drunken Charlie brak's neck-bane;
And through the whins, and by the cairn,
Whare hunters fand the murder'd bairn;
And near the thorn, aboon the well,
Whare Mungo's mither hang'd hersel.
Before him Doon pours all his floods;
The doubling storm roars through the
woods;
The lightnings flash from pole to pole;
Near and more near the thunders roll:
When, glimmering through the groaning
trees,
Kirk-Alloway seem'd in a bleeze,
Through ilka bore the beams were glanc-
ing,
And loud resounding mirth and dancing.

Inspiring, bold John Barleycorn!
What dangers thou canst make us scorn!
Wi' tippenny, we fear nae evil;
Wi' usquabae, we'll face the Devil!
The swats sae ream'd in Tammie's noddle,
Fair play, he car'd na deils a boddle.
But Maggie stood, right sair astonish'd,
Till, by the heel and hand admonish'd,
She ventur'd forward on the light;
And, wow! Tam saw an unco sight!

Warlocks and witches in a dance;
Nae cotillion, brent new frae France,

But hornpipes, jigs, strathspeys and reels,
Put life and mettle in their heels.
A winnock-bunker in the east,
There sat Auld Nick, in shape o' beast;
A touzie tyke, black, grim and large,
To gie them music was his charge;
He screw'd the pipes and gart them skirl,
Till roof and rafters a' did dirl.
Coffins stood round, like open presses,
That shaw'd the dead in their last dresses;
And, by some devilish cantraip sleight,
Each in its cauld hand held a light;
By which heroic Tam was able
To note upon the haly table,
A murderer's banes, in gibbet-airns;
Twa span-lang, wee, unchristen'd bairns;
A theif new-cutted frae a rape—
Wi' his last gasp his gab did gape;
Five tomahawks wi' bluid red-rusted;
Five scymitars wi' murder crusted;
A garter which a babe had strangled;
A knife a father's throat had mangled—
Whom his ain son o' life bereft—
The grey hairs yet stack to the heft;
Wi' mair of horrible and awefu',
Which ev'n to name wad be unlawfu'.
Three Lawyers' tongues, turned inside
out,
Wi' lies seamed life a beggar's clout;
Three Priests' hearts, rotten, black as
muck,
Lay stinking, vile, in every neuk.

    As Tammie glowr'd, amaz'd and curi-
ous,
The mirth and fun grew fast and furious;
The piper loud and louder blew,
The dancers quick and quicker flew,
They reel'd, they set, they cross'd, they
cleekit,
Till ilka carlin swat and reekit,
And coost her duddies to the wark,
And linket at it in her sark!

    Now Tam, O Tam! had thae been
queans,
A' plump and strapping in their teens!
Their sarks, instead o' creeshie flannen,
Been snaw-white seventeen hunder
linen!—
Thir breeks o' mine, my only pair,

That ance were plush, o' guid blue hair,
I wad hae gi'en them off my hurdies
For ae blink o' the bonie burdies!

    But wither'd beldams, auld and droll,
Rigwoodie hags wad spean a foal,
Louping and flinging on a crummock,
I wonder did na turn thy stomach!

    But Tam kend what was what fu'
brawlie:
There was ae winsome wench and
wawlie,
That night enlisted in the core,
Lang after kend on Carrick shore:
(For monie a beast to dead she shot,
An' perish'd monie a bonie boat,
And shook baith meikle corn and bear,
And held the country-side in fear.)
Her cutty sark, o' Paisley harn,
That while a lassie she had worn,
In longitude though sorely scanty,
It was her best, and she was vauntie....
Ah! little kend thy reverend grannie,
That sark she coft for her wee Nannie,
Wi' twa pund Scots ('twas a' her riches),
Wad ever grac'd a dance of witches!

    But here my Muse her wing maun
cour,
Sic flights as far beyond her power:
To sing how Nannie lap and flang
(A souple jade she was and strang);
And how Tam stood like ane bewitch'd,
And thought his very een enrich'd;
Even Satan glowr'd, and fidg'd fu' fain,
And hotch'd and blew wi' might and
main;
Till first ae caper, syne anither,
Tam tint his reason a' thegither,
And roars out: 'Weel done, Cutty-sark!'
And in an instant all was dark;
And scarcely had he Maggie rallied,
When out the hellish legion sallied.

    As bees bizz out wi' angry fyke,
When plundering herds assail their byke;
As open pussie's mortal foes,
When, pop! she starts before their nose;
As eager runs the market-crowd,
When 'Catch the thief!' resounds aloud:

So Maggie runs, the witches folow,
Wi' monie an eldritch skriech and hol-
low.

    Ah, Tam! Ah, Tam! thou'll get thy
fairin!
In hell they'll roast thee like a herrin!
In vain thy Kate awaits thy comin!
Kate soon will be a woefu' woman!
Now, do thy speedy utmost, Meg,
And win the key-stane of the brig;
There, at them thou thy tail may toss,
A running stream they dare na cross!
But ere the key-stane she could make,
The fient a tail she had to shake;
For Nannie, far before the rest,
Hard upon noble Maggie prest,
And flew at Tam wi furious ettle;
But little wist she Maggie's mettle!
Ae spring brought off her master hale,
But left behind her ain grey tail:
The carlin claught her by the rump,
And left poor Maggie scarce a stump.

    Now, wha this tale o' truth shall read,
Ilk man and mother's son, take heed:
Whene'er to drink you are inclin'd,
Or cutty sarks run in your mind,
Think! ye may buy the joys o'er dear:
Remember Tam o' Shanter's meare.

A Toast To The Lassies
by Granpaw

In the Broon hoose we hae four fine examples of wumminkind.

To Maggie with your braw wee face – and your fine singing voice:

> I see her in the dewy flowers—
> I see her sweet and fair.
> I hear her in the tunefu' birds—
> I hear her charm the air.

And if she puts her rollers in she has lovely curly hair!

To Daphne, a big lassie with an even bigger heart.

> Fair fa' your honest sonsie face
> The nicest lassie of a' your race
> You like a bit of haddock and a wee bit of plaice
> And a wee roll an' chips if you've still got the space.

To Maw – whit a rerr spread – yer a wee gem.

> Maw Broon, she swears, that stovies is
> Her bestest work, she classes, O:
> Her prentice han' she try'd on mince,
> An' then she made the tatties, O.

And to my best wee pal, the Bairn.

> My favourite hoose in a' the toon
> Is Glebe Street, number 10,
> For there the bonniest lassie lives,
> My wee darlin': the Bairn.

A toast to you all – Scotland's finest – I am proud to be your Granpaw! As Rabbie Burns said – and he sent a thing or twa aboot the lassies –

> Auld Nature swears, the lovely dears
> Her noblest work she classes, O:
> Her prentice han' she try'd on man,
> An' then she made the lasses, O.

GREEN GROW THE RASHES, O

There's nought but care on ev'ry han',
  In every hour that passes, O:
What signifies the life o' man,
  An' 'twere na for the lasses, O?

Green grow the rashes, O;
Green grow the rashes, O;
The sweetest hours that e'er I spend,
Are spent among the lasses, O.

The war'ly race may riches chase,
  An' riches still may fly them, O;
An' though at last they catch them fast,
  Their hearts can ne'er enjoy them, O.

But gie me a cannie hour at e'en,
  My arms about my dearie, O;
An' war'ly cares an' war'ly men
  May a' gae tapsalteerie, O!

For you sae douce, ye sneer at this;
  Ye're nought but senseless asses, O;
The wisest man the warl' e'er saw,
  He dearly lov'd the lasses, O.

Auld Nature swears, the lovely dears
  Her noblest work she classes, O:
Her prentice han' she try'd on man,
  An' then she made the lasses, O.

THE REPLY
by Maggie

The Broons Lassies are rather outnumbered by oor male relatives. Apologies to the memory of Robert Burns, and following Granpaw's lead, I've written a wee poem about you all. It's almost as bad as Granpaw's.

Starting with youngest, first we have the Twins
Is there ony kind o' trouble they hivnae been in?
Ae Twin breaks a windae ... tther Twin gets the blame.
Perhaps they widna be so naughty if we ca'ed them by their names?

Horace — who is so brainy — head always in a book,
Take my advice — short trousers are a bad look.
You're brighter than the rest of us — you always do us proud,
You'll be successful with the lassies when long trousers are allowed.

Joe, my big strong brither, with the squarest jaw in toon
I think we are agreed you are the best lookin' Broon. (Apart from me!)
Your partner in crime is Hen, the tallest man you'll ever see.
Why you never became a pole vaulter is a mystery to me.

My Paw — a careful man it's true — especially with his money.
Where would we be without him? Life would be much less funny.
He's been a fine support to Maw and great father you'll agree,
Not bad for a man who is only 5 foot 3. *I am 5 foot 6!!*

Granpaw, our oldest Broon, at heart is a big wean
But you'll never hear us saying the auld scunner is a pain! Oh no! *(Not within earshot anyway.)*
You've always got some scheme that gets us running to your aid,
Then we find out when we get there that it's all been a charade.

The Broon men — you must agree — fine specimens one and all:
One is brainy, two are cheeky, some are short, one is tall.
Please, ladies, let us have a toast, just like we did before,
"Boys: without you we'd have less work to do but life would be a bore."

The Rights Of Woman

Spoken by Miss Fontanelle† on her
Benefit Night, November 26, 1792

ROBERT BURNS

WHILE Europe's eye is fix'd on mighty things,
The fate of Empires and the fall of Kings;
While quacks of State must each produce his plan,
And even children lisp the Rights of Man;
Amid this mighty fuss just let me mention,
The Rights of Woman merit some attention.

    First, in the Sexes' intermix'd connection,
One sacred Right of Woman is, *protection*.—
The tender flower that lifts its head, elate,
Helpless, must fall before the blasts of Fate,
Sunk on the earth, defac'd its lovely form,
Unless your shelter ward th' impending storm.

    Our second Right—but needless here is caution,
To keep that right inviolate's the fashion;
Each man of sense has it so full before him,
He'd die before he'd wrong it—'tis *decorum*.—
There was, indeed, in far less polish'd days,
A time, when rough rude man had naughty ways,
Would swagger, swear, get drunk, kick up a riot,

Nay even thus invade a Lady's quiet.
Now, thank our stars! those Gothic times are fled,
Now, well-bred men—and you are all well-bred—
Most justly think (and we are much the gainers)
Such conduct neither spirit, wit, nor manners.

    For Right the third, our last, our best, our dearest,
That right to fluttering female hearts the nearest;
Which even the Rights of Kings, in low prostration,
Most humbly own—'tis dear, dear *admiration*!
In that blest sphere alone we live and move;
There taste that life of life—immortal love.
Smiles, glances, sighs, tears, fits, flirtations, airs;
'Gainst such an host what flinty savage dares,
When awful Beauty joins with all her charms—
Who is so rash as rise in rebel arms?

    But truce with kings, and truce with constitutions,
With bloody armaments and revolutions;
Let Majesty your first attention summon,
Ah! ca ira! THE MAJESTY OF WOMAN!

† Miss Fontanelle was a favourite actress in Dumfries

Caramel Shortbread

A tray of shortbread
1 large tin condensed milk
(400 g/14 oz)
200g/ 7 oz chocolate

The day before you make the shortbread, place a tin of condensed milk, pierced at the top, in a pan of water, bring to the boil and then simmer over a medium heat for two hours. Remove from the heat and leave overnight.

Make the shortbread (your usual recipe). Allow to cool in the tray. Spread caramelised condensed milk over the uncut shortbread once cooled. Melt the chocolate and spread over the caramel. Slice before it is completely cool, then leave in a cool place for the toppings to set.

✂ cut here

Tablet - A rich, sweet treat

200 g/8 oz condensed milk
50 g/2 oz butter
1 kg/2 lb sugar
1 cup milk
Vanilla essence (optional)

Bring the ingredients to the boil slowly in a large thick-bottomed saucepan and stir regularly. After a few minutes, test consistency by dropping a little of the mixture into cold water (it should be like soft putty), or use a sugar thermometer and stop heating when it reaches 240°F/108°C (soft ball). Remove from the heat and beat with a wooden spoon until the mixture begins to solidify. Pour into a greased tray and cut into bars.

Housewife Weekly "cut out and keep" Scottish Recipes

No.25

Shortbread

500 g/1 lb butter, softened
175 g/7 oz caster sugar
600 g/1 1/4 lb plain flour, sieved (crunchier biscuits can be made by substituting 50 g/ 2 oz semolina for 50 g /2 oz plain flour)

Preheat the oven to 160°C/325°F/gas mark 3. Beat together the butter and the sugar. Beat in the flour and semolina, 100 g/ 4 oz at a time, until smooth. If the dough becomes too stiff to stir, knead in the rest of the flour with your hands. Grease and flour a large baking tray. Roll out the dough and press into the baking sheet. Mark the dough into fingers or pie-shaped wedges and prick the pieces all over with the prongs of a fork. Bake in the centre of the oven for 30 to 40 minutes or until firm to the touch. Makes about two dozen biscuits.

ADDRESS TO THE TOOTHACHE

Robert Burns

MY curse upon your venom'd stang,
That shoots my tortur'd gums alang,
An' thro' my lug gies mony a twang,
    Wi' gnawing vengeance,
Tearing my nerves wi' bitter pang,
    Like racking engines!

A' down my beard the slavers trickle,
I throw the wee stools o'er the mickle,
While round the fire the giglets keckle,
    To see me loup,
While, raving mad, I wish a heckle
    Were i' their doup!

When fevers burn, or ague freezes,
Rheumatics gnaw, or cholic squeezes,
Our neebour's sympathy can ease us,
    Wi' pitying moan;
But thee—thou hell o' a' diseases—
    Aye mocks our groan.

O a' the numerous human dools,
Ill hairsts, daft bargains, cutty-stools,
Or worthy frien's rak'd i' the mools—
    Sad sight to see!
The tricks o' knaves, or fash o' fools,
    Thou bear'st the gree!

Where'er that place be priests ca' hell,
Where a' the tones o' misery yell,
An' ranked plagues their numbers tell,
    In dreadfu' raw,
Thou, TOOTHACHE, surely bear'st the bell,
    Amang them a'!

O thou grim, mischief-making chiel,
That gars the notes o' discord squeel,
Till daft mankind aft dance a reel
    In gore, a shoe-thick,
Gie a' the faes o' Scotland's weal
    A TOWNMOND'S TOOTHACHE!

Sweet Milk Scones

½ lb. flour
½ oz. sugar
1 oz. butter
1 tsp cream of tartar
½ tsp bicarbonate of soda
½ tsp salt
¼ pint milk

Rub the butter into the flour. Keep your hands cool and keep the mixing of this as light as possible. What I mean by that is see if you can get as much air into the mixture as possible. Add the rest of the dry ingredients, and mix into a light dough with the milk. Turn the dough out on to a floured board. Handle it as little as possible. Roll it out lightly and cut in eight pieces. Lay on a greased baking tray. Glaze the scones with a brush of egg or milk. Bake in a hot oven for 10 minutes.

DROP SCONES

1 lb flour
1 teaspoon bicarbonate of soda
1 teaspoon cream of tartar
½ teaspoon salt
2 oz caster sugar or syrup
2 eggs
Milk or buttermilk to mix

Combine all the dry ingredients. Beat the eggs and add to a well in the centre of dry mixture. Mix with as much milk as you need to make a soft, smooth batter. Grease a hot girdle with fat (don't use butter - it will burn). Drop a spoonful of the mixture on to the girdle with a metal spoon. When brown on one side, turn and brown on the other. Leave to cool on a wire tray and wrap in a clean tea towel. Serve with butter and home made jam or golden syrup. Delicious hot or cold.

THE STAR O' RABBIE BURNS

Words by James Thomson.
Music by James Booth.

There is a star whose beaming ray
Is shed on ev'ry clime.
It shines by night, it shines by day
And ne'er grows dim wi' time.
It rose upon the banks of Ayr,
It shone on Doon's clear stream —
A hundred years are gane and mair,
Yet brighter grows its beam.

Chorus
Let kings and courtiers rise and fa',
This world has mony turns
But brightly beams aboon them a'
The star o' Rabbie Burns.

Though he was but a ploughman lad
And wore the hodden grey,
Auld Scotland's sweetest bard was bred
Aneath a roof o' strae.
To sweep the strings o' Scotia's lyre,
It needs nae classic lore;
It's mither wit an native fire
That warms the bosom's core.

Chorus

On fame's emblazon'd page enshrin'd
His name is foremost now,
And many a costly wreath's been twin'd
To grace his honest brow.
And Scotland's heart expands wi' joy
Whene'er the day returns
That gave the world its peasant boy
Immortal Rabbie Burns.

Chorus

AULD LANG SYNE

Should auld acquaintance be forgot,
　　And never brought to mind?
Should auld acquaintance be forgot,
　　And days o' lang syne?

CHORUS

For auld lang syne, my jo,
　　For auld lang syne,
We'll tak a cup o' kindness yet,
　　For auld lang syne.

And surely ye'll be your pint-stowp!
　　And surely I'll be mine!
And we'll tak a cup o' kindness yet,
　　For auld lang syne.

We twa hae run about the braes
　　And pu'd the gowans fine;
But we've wander'd monie a weary foot
　　Sin' auld lang syne.

We twa hae paidl'd i' the burn,
　　Frae mornin' sun till dine;
But seas between us braid hae roar'd
　　Sin' auld lang syne.

And there's a hand, my trusty fiere!
　　And gie's a hand o' thine!
And we'll tak a right guid-willie
waught,
　　For auld lang syne.